Grow Old With Me

Grow Old With Me

ART AND NARRATIVE BY Lucy Rose Fischer

Temuna Press
MINNEAPOLIS, 2019

ISBN 978-1-7335091-2-1

Library of Congress Control Number: 2019904768

9 8 7 6 5 4 3 2 1
First Edition

Printed in the United States of America

Book design: Sarah Miner
Author photo and art photography: Sid Konikoff
Published by Temuna Press, Minneapolis

Distributed by:
Itasca Books
5120 Cedar Lake Road
Minneapolis, MN 55416
Phones: 952-345-4488/1-800-901-3480
Fax: 952-920-0541

Copies of this book can be ordered at:
www.lucyrosedesigns.com

To Mark

Did you take your pill before bedtime, my love?

Is the front door locked?

Are you sure?

Are you feeling chilly?

Do you need another blanket?

How did we get to be so old?

BEFORE . . .

When you are ten, you have a cherry-red Schwinn
one-speed bicycle. You are an explorer,
peddling fast down every street
to see what is there.
You're a dreamer.

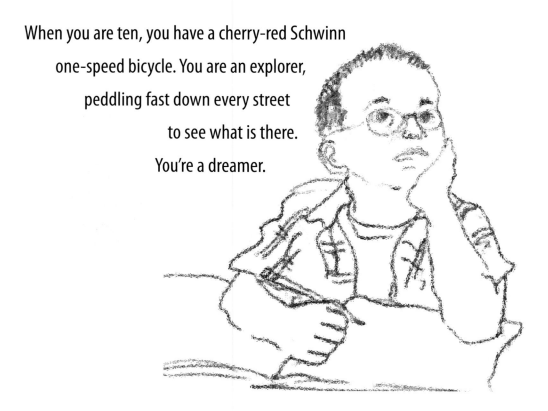

You are a shy boy who loves numbers. When you go to summer camp,
you don't learn how to swim. Instead you learn to play chess.

When I'm ten, I have double ponytails.
I sit on the edge of my bed
and write little poems with rhymes.
I sprawl on the living room carpet
and draw pictures.
I love to daydream.

WHEN WE MEET . . .

We're young. We think we're grown up.

You're nineteen years old, a sophomore.

You're shy.

I'm eighteen—a new freshman.

I'm shy too.

But I like to flirt a little.

The university is a whirlwind of books,

science, art, culture . . . and SEX.

All those sex hormones hover in the air.

We become a couple—holding hands all around campus, eating and talking, talking and chewing, giggling in the library.

We fall in LIKE.
Then in LOVE.

My parents are wary.

"She's too young to get so serious."

Your parents are suspicious.

"What do we know about this girl?"

THE WEDDING

The planning is convoluted, complicated and a little traumatic.

I drown in a sea of details:

Who gets invited?

Who doesn't?

Who wears chartreuse or navy or cerise?

What flowers?

What photos?

I ask your opinion on flowers, photos, colors . . .

"Whatever," you say.

On the day before the wedding, a blizzard arrives.

The guests come anyway—their cars plunging through mounds of snow.

We're NEWLYWEDS.

We share:

* a bed
* bodily fluids
* viruses
* our random thoughts and most profound ideas
* food from one another's plates
* bank accounts
* our love and our passions

We have MOODS.

When you're angry, you're a snail—silent and withdrawn.

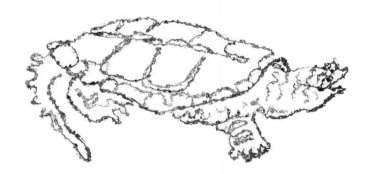

I'm a snapping turtle. I might bite your head off.

Sometimes we're both in a mood . . . we're like porcupines . . .

We stay away from each other.

Our home has LONG ARMS to welcome friends, neighbors, and our family . . .

When we make new friends, we invite them to dinner.

We are a team: I cook and you clean up.

I make concoctions from whatever I find in the refrigerator—I call it "refrigerator cooking." Our guests never know what to expect.

It's BABY TIME

Our best friends are having a baby. We watch as our girlfriend's body grows large.

Our friends bring home their lovely baby.

Another couple is pregnant.

    Then another and another.

        Everybody's doing it.

            We feel estranged from this world of babies.

So—what to do?

The little circle of birth control pills goes out with the trash.

Sex with a purpose now.

I get nauseous.

Certain odors and even noises make me woozy and seasick.

I'm pregnant.

At first, no one can tell. My tummy is flat. I walk around with a secret.

Now I look pregnant.

I'm BIG

bigger than a MACK TRUCK

bigger than a RHINOCEROS

I'm late—overdue.

Will this baby ever come?

We rush to the hospital with our carefully packed bag and camera.

False labor. We go home.

Two hours later, we rush back to the hospital with bag and camera.

I'm lying on a hospital bed with no contractions, not even a pinch or a whisper.

We go home.

Will this baby ever come?

Then I'm in labor—really in labor in the middle of the night. I'm up on all fours, rocking to manage the pain, which will not be managed.

We rush to the hospital—bag and camera left behind. A crescendo of pain. I'm in love with the smiling nurse who massages my back. I don't even know her name.

Into the glare of fluorescent hospital lights, **BABY** emerges.

You see **BABY** first. "It's a boy!"

You are crying.

Then I'm crying.

BABY is crying.

Baby is brilliant.

He knows how to suckle on my breast.

I'm **MOTHER** now. I wear clothes with zippers or buttons down the front.

I look at cows with kinship—

sisters in milkship.

I'm taking a walk one day, pushing the carriage,

when my milk begins to *GUSH*—

two round wet moons on my peach-colored front-zipper dress.

Our quiet and orderly life explodes.

Nights and days are jumbled.

Our living room is a playroom.

Our baby morphs into LITTLE BOY.

This happens all at once, when we're not looking.

LITTLE BOY has tantrums.

I cut up a banana for him.

"No!" he screams and pounds his little fists.

"I want the banana whole!"

This is the humpty-dumpty tantrum

when all the King's horses and all the King's men

can't put the banana back together again.

LITTLE BOY is five years old.

You and I engage in **high-level negotiations** over the dinner table:

* ✳ who will pick up Little Boy

* ✳ who will buy milk on the way home

* ✳ who will vacuum the shag carpet . . .

Our family life is a juggling act.

LITTLE BOY goes to school.

He learns to read.

He's good at arithmetic, like his dad.

$$17 + 28 = 476$$

$$248 \div 32 = 7.75$$

He rides his bike all over town.

Little boy becomes a Cub Scout.

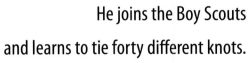

He joins the Boy Scouts
and learns to tie forty different knots.

We are MIDDLE AGE!

We have our careers.

We are high-wire artists.

There are grand times, when the world applauds,

and awful times, when we fall

down

down

down.

We take turns holding a net—to catch one another.

Sometimes we're together but not really together.

Each of us has a head stuffed with random thoughts, ideas for projects . . .

Our house chases after us with a million TASKS…

* water the garden

* vacuum

* fix the porch railing

* pay the bills

* change the kitchen light bulb

* change the sheets

* paint the living room

* do the laundry

* clean the toilets

* walk the dog

We've come to know one another so well, it's as if we have X-RAY vision. We can see inside each other.

When I hear you turn the key in the front door, I know how you're feeling. "What's wrong?" I ask.

You can fall asleep at nine o'clock in the evening.

I want to talk at night.

"Not now," you mumble, your eyes already closing.

I lean against my pillow and read a novel. You are deeper and deeper into sleep,

sounding like a creaking door, an old-fashioned upright vacuum cleaner,

the rumbling of a tiger.

When we're both asleep, there is no one to witness our fugue of snores,

except perhaps the dog, who also snores.

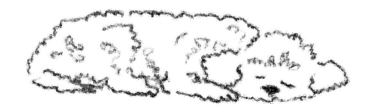

At five am, you get up to go to the gym. You hear my buzz saw snores.

You have a keen sense of direction. You find your way by instinct—as if guided by some magnetic force.

I get lost without you. If there's a choice—to turn right or turn left—I usually pick the wrong way.

You lose THINGS—keys, wallet, cell phone . . . I hear you running around the house, upstairs, downstairs . . . "Where is my . . .?"

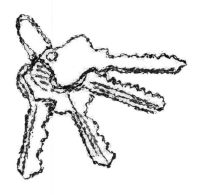

I have an instinctive talent.

In a few moments: "Here is your cell phone . . ." or wallet or papers or keys or . . .

When we're in the car together and you're driving, I make helpful comments.

"There's a stop sign . . . the light is turning . . . watch out for that car . . ."

Even if I don't say a word, I press my foot to the floor, slamming my invisible brakes.

"You're driving me crazy," you say.

We see the marriages of some of our friends fly apart.

Sometimes it's a surprise. Sometimes it isn't.

How do we know what happens in the hearts of even good friends?

I wonder, *Could this happen to us?*

I think you wonder too.

But we don't talk about it.

Every now and then, we fight—really argue.

We stab each other with accusations dipped in blood.

You go into your study and don't say a word.

I want to crawl into a little space and never come out.

Then one of us, you or I, walks over to the other:

"I'm sorry . . ."

"I'm sorry too. I don't want to fight with you . . ."

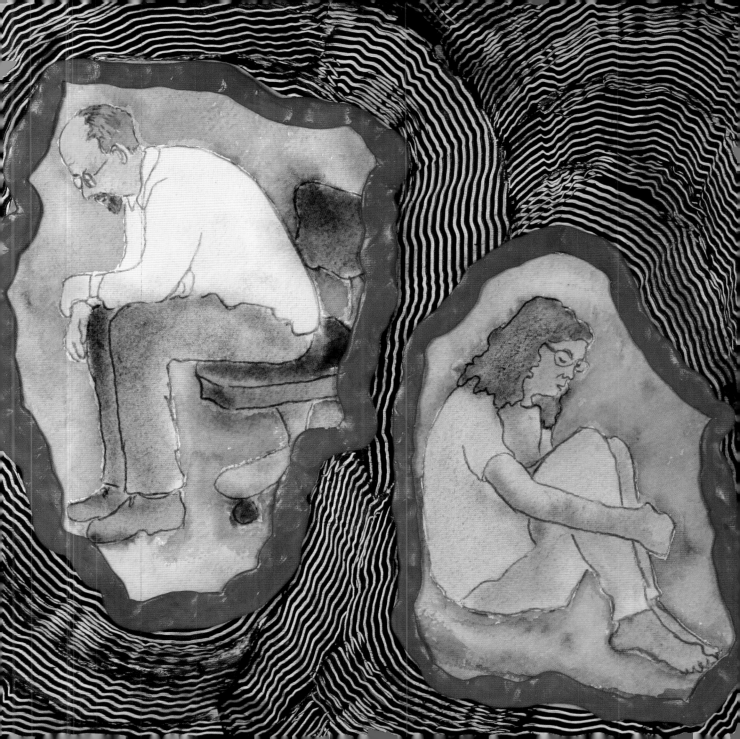

Sometimes I worry about you.

It's a little past six one evening. I wonder, *What time did you say you'd be home?*

Dinner is ready on the stove.

A shimmer of fear ruffles around my head.

Now it's 6:47 pm. You really are late.

What did you say this morning? I can't remember.

I sit on the blue couch and listen to sleet hitting the windows.

My worry widens into a large looming beast perched over my head.

I play the what-if game. *What if something has happened . . .*

Then I see the glow of your headlights coming up the driveway.

A quick kiss.

You say, "There was a pileup on the highway. I was worried you would worry."

Our son—who used to be LITTLE BOY—gets married.

The wedding is outdoors, in a garden where the ground is covered with small stones.
We dance and dance all night.

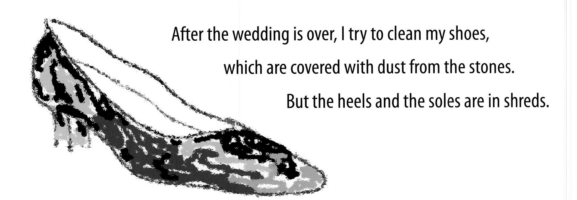

After the wedding is over, I try to clean my shoes,
which are covered with dust from the stones.
But the heels and the soles are in shreds.

"Look," I tell you, "I've worn out my new shoes dancing at our son's wedding."
"Isn't that wonderful!" you say.

We go to

OREGON ITALY CALIFORNIA HAWAII

CANADA INDONESIA CHINA WASHINGTON ENGLAND

PORTUGAL NEVADA ICELAND ILLINOIS AUSTRIA NEW YORK

WISCONSIN FRANCE ROMANIA MAINE TENNESSEE

ISRAEL FLORIDA UTAH TURKEY SERBIA CROATIA

GEORGIA CZECHOSLOVAKIA POLAND

As soon as we get home from one trip, you ask,

"Where are we going next—and when?"

We're at a resort in a tropical country.

I'm sitting by the swimming pool with my glasses off, and I notice a balding older man standing on the other side of the pool. His pale-pink flesh bulges a little over his striped bathing trunks.

Suddenly I realize—"That older man is *YOU*."

One night, after a difficult day, we're lying in bed, and I say something silly.

Or maybe you make one of your outrageous jokes.

We start to giggle—bubbles of laughter float in the air.

It's time to sleep, but we are laughing and laughing.

Like little children, we can't stop . . .

The next morning, we can't remember what was so funny.

We're growing older, but we still have our DREAMS.

Ever since I was a little girl, art was something I loved.

Now, I'm old enough to follow my dream. I launch a new career as an artist.
I teach myself to paint *upside down*, *inside out*, and *backwards* on handblown glass.

I show my art in exhibits and occasionally manage to sell some of my creations.
I litter our home with my painted glass vases and bowls in vivid colors.

You love to give tours of my art to friends and strangers.

You decide to take cello lessons.

"Why the cello?" I ask.

"It's the most beautiful instrument," you say with a sigh.

But not the easiest.

A friend tells you, "You have to practice for 10,000 hours to be any good."

"Okay," you say, "I'll practice one hour a day. So, I'll be a good musician by the time I'm 118 years old!"

I take long walks when you practice the cello.

Our son and his bride have children.

We now have splendid grandchildren with cheeks like peaches
and enough energy to light the world.

But they live far away, and so we visit.

At bedtime, we sit with our grandchildren and tell them stories about our lives
from long ago. Our stories are like lessons in ancient history.

Life is fragile.

One day you get sick. You have a fever. You're hot. You're cold.

Is it the flu?

I take you to urgent care. Standing in line, you can't stop shaking.

The doctor says to me, "Your husband has a serious infection. He needs to go to the hospital."

Your fever spikes to 104 degrees. You're delirious. The doctor in the hospital asks you simple questions. You have a blank look and can't answer.

You're in the hospital for five days with tubes sprouting from your body. After IV antibiotics and fluids, you slowly get better.

I'm terrified. I might have lost you.

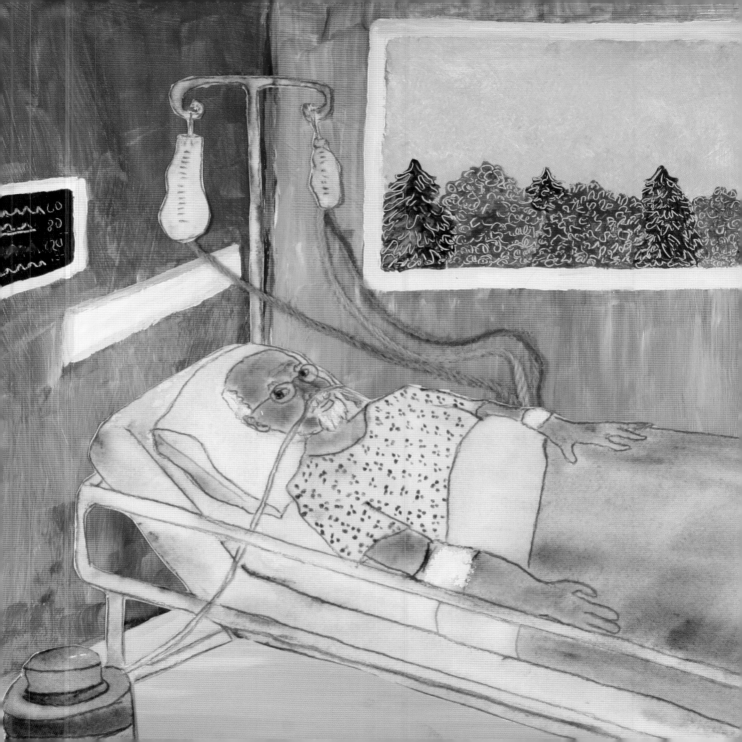

Our home is crowded now with SWEET GHOSTS: my parents, your parents, and other relatives and friends who were dear to us and have gone to the "other side."

Our memories are vivid and rich:

* my mother offering a slice of her yeast coffee cake
* my father surprising a child with his handshake trick
* your dad, with a prayer shawl over his shoulders, saying his morning prayers
* your mother, with eyes sparkling, showing us her new paintings
* Aunt Irene planting red lip marks on our cheeks
* our friend Gary taking seven-minute naps
* your cousin Milton insisting life is long, not short
* our friend Ab asking questions that no one can answer
* Jerry telling us his wonderful stories . . .

We live with our ghosts, whose faces we conjure, whose voices resound in our heads.

We've been together for more than half a century.

We were so young when we met—propelled by our raging teenage hormones.

How has it happened that our love has lasted all these years?

We are like

gibbons

macaroni penguins

barn owls

albatrosses

bald eagles

French angelfish

All species that mate for life!

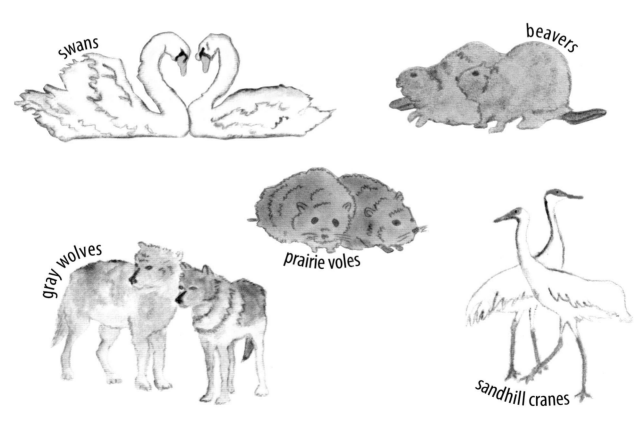

swans

beavers

prairie voles

gray wolves

sandhill cranes

Our marriage is a very long conversation, which continues, moment after moment, year after year.

We talk about everyday plans . . . the weather report . . . what movie to see . . . the grocery list . . .

We share our problems . . . our dreams . . . our love . . .

We figure out stuff together.

We talk about politics . . . religion . . . philosophy . . . books . . . art . . .

We laugh at each other's jokes.

We console one another when we're feeling down.

We celebrate our small triumphs and victories.

The long tangles of our words embrace us and bind us in love.

... I really ... When you ... I was frightened ... It was difficult for both of us to ... One moment I felt ... I couldn't breathe ... If you hadn't jumped ... How can we explain ...

... This time ... I felt uneasy because ... what happened was ...

Tell me about you ... When we went ...
... I saw ... This took my breath away ...
... I'm sorry ... Yesterday he said ... I'm having a
... problem ... Have you ever wondered ... How do they ...
... Everytime we go there ... In the morning I was so ...
... I was shocked but not really ... told me ... Really ...
... and I felt ... Tell me about you ... Let's do
... You seemed ... Look at this ...
... How do they ... Listen I'm feeling ... Listen to ...
... It yesterday or the day before ... Was
... and cried ... Wait til you hear ... I cried
... was awful ... By the way ... That
... knows about ... Don't forget to ... Did y...
... I read about ... I just he...
... not sure ... Tell...

As we grow older, we look at one another with tender trepidation.

How many more years together?

How many good years?

grow old with me.

Acknowledgments

A good marriage is a mystery. I feel extraordinarily lucky to have found Mark, who has been my love and partner for more than half a century. He was wary when I began working on this book about our marriage. What secrets would I reveal? What would I say about him? Nonetheless, he helped edit this book—with patience, insight and without censorship.

Many thanks also to Megan Marsnik, Lydia Roth-Laube and Melpomeni Murdakes for their helpful reviews and commentary, to Mary Kierstadt for copyediting, to Sid Konikoff for photography, to Sarah Miner for interior and cover design, to Rachel Holscher for project management at Bookmobile, and to Rachel Anderson for help with marketing and publicity.

Lucy Rose Fischer, PhD, is an award-winning Minnesota artist, author, and sociologist.

As an artist, Lucy Rose specializes in creating fanciful and colorful designs on glass—painting upside-down, inside-out and backwards on hand blown glass. Her art has been shown in numerous exhibits and is on permanent display in public settings and private collections. She and her art are featured on the Twin Cities Public Television documentaries *The Creative Power of Aging* and *Life Changing Art*.

She is the author of four previously published books. Her most recent book, *I'm New at Being Old*, received a Midwest Book Award and an Independent Publishers Gold Award.

Before launching her art career, she had a distinguished 25-year career as a researcher, directing studies and publishing books and research articles on aging and family. She is a Fellow of the Gerontological Society of America for "outstanding achievement and exemplary contributions to the field of aging."

www.lucyrosedesigns.com

Life is a work of art.
Art is a work of life.